TIME TRAVEL GUIDES

MEDIEVAL EUROPE

John Haywood

Chicago, Illinois

Designed by Clare Nicholas
Photo research by Amy Sparks
Illustrations by Peter Bull
Printed and bound in China by Leo
    Paper Group

12 11 10 09 08
10 9 8 7 6 5 4 3 2 1

Library of Congress Cataloging-in-Publication Data
Haywood, John, 1956-
    Medieval Europe / John Haywood.
    p. cm. – (Time travel guide)
    Includes bibliographical references and index.
    ISBN 978-1-4109-2909-9 (hardcover) – ISBN 978-1-
    4109-2915-0 (pbk.)
    1. Civilization, Medieval–Juvenile literature. 2. Europe–
Civilization–Juvenile literature. I. Title.
    CB351.H38 2007
    940.1–dc22
                                        2007005625

Acknowledgments
The publishers would like to thank the following
for permission to reproduce photographs (t = top,
b= bottom):
AKG pp. 11 (b) (British Library), 14 (British Library),
17 (British Library), 18 (Bibliothèque Nationale, Paris),
30 (Herve Champollion), 31, 36 (British Library), 40
(British Library), 45 (British Library), 47 (Bibliothèque
Nationale, Paris), 48–49 (Jost Schilgen); Art Archive
pp. 26 (Palazzo Pubblico, Siena/Dagli Orti), 34 (Musée
Condé Chantilly/ Dagli Orti), 37 (Corbis/Alfredo Dagli
Orti), 53 (Bibliothèque Municipale, Moulins/Dagli Orti);
Bridgeman Art Library pp. 8 (Musée de l'Oeuvre de Nôtre
Dame, Strasbourg, France/Giraudon), 11 (t) (Biblioteca
Monasterio del Escorial, Madrid, Spain/Giraudon), 15
(Rheinisches Landesmuseum, Bonn, Germany/Giraudon),
19 (Museum of London, UK), 21 (Bibliothèque
Municipale, Cambrai, France/Giraudon), 23 (Museum
of London, UK), 38 (Palazzo Pubblico, Siena, Italy/
Alinari), 41 (Osterreichische Nationalbibliothek, Vienna,
Austria/Alinari), 42 (Musée de la Tapisserie, Bayeux,
France/With special authorization of the city of Bayeux/
Giraudon), 44 (Osterreichische Nationalbibliothek,
Vienna, Austria/Alinari), 51 (Bibliothèque Nationale,
Paris, France/Archives Charmet), 52 (Glasgow University
Library, Scotland); Corbis pp. 6–7 (Michael Busselle),
12 (Patrick Ward), 28 (Karl-Josef Hildenbrand/dpa),
54–55 (Elio Ciol); John Haywood pp. 24–25.

Cover photograph of Arundel Castle, Arundel, West
Sussex, England, courtesy of Adam van Bunnens/
Alamy. Photograph of a detail of the Super Decretales
Manuscript (ca. 1300–1399) courtesy of the Museum
of Biblioteca Capitular Tortosa/Ramon Manent/Corbis.
Photograph of a 13th-century ivory carving of knight
from a chess set courtesy of The Art Archive/Corbis.

The publishers would like to thank Dr. Susan Edgington
for her assistance in the preparation of this book.

Disclaimer
All the Internet addresses (URLs) given in this book were
valid at the time of going to press. However, due to the
dynamic nature of the Internet, some addresses may
have changed, or sites may have changed or ceased to
exist since publication. While the author and publishers
regret any inconvenience this may cause readers, no
responsibility for any such changes can be accepted by
either the author or the publishers.

CONTENTS

Words that appear in the text in bold, **like this**, are explained in the glossary.

Pilgrimage destinations
Universities

KINGDOM OF NORWAY

KINGDOM OF SCOTLAND

IRELAND

KINGDOM OF DENMARK

ATLANTIC OCEAN

KINGDOM OF ENGLAND

Oxford

London

Canterbury

Nôtre Dame

PRINCIPALITY OF WALES

Pilgrim cross

NORMANDY

Paris

Santiago de Compostela

KINGDOM OF NAVARRE

KINGDOM OF FRANCE

HOLY ROMAN EMPIRE

KINGDOM OF LEON

KINGDOM OF PORTUGAL

KINGDOM OF CASTILE

KINGDOM OF ARAGON

Bologna

Rome

MUSLIM STATES

MEDITERRANEAN SEA

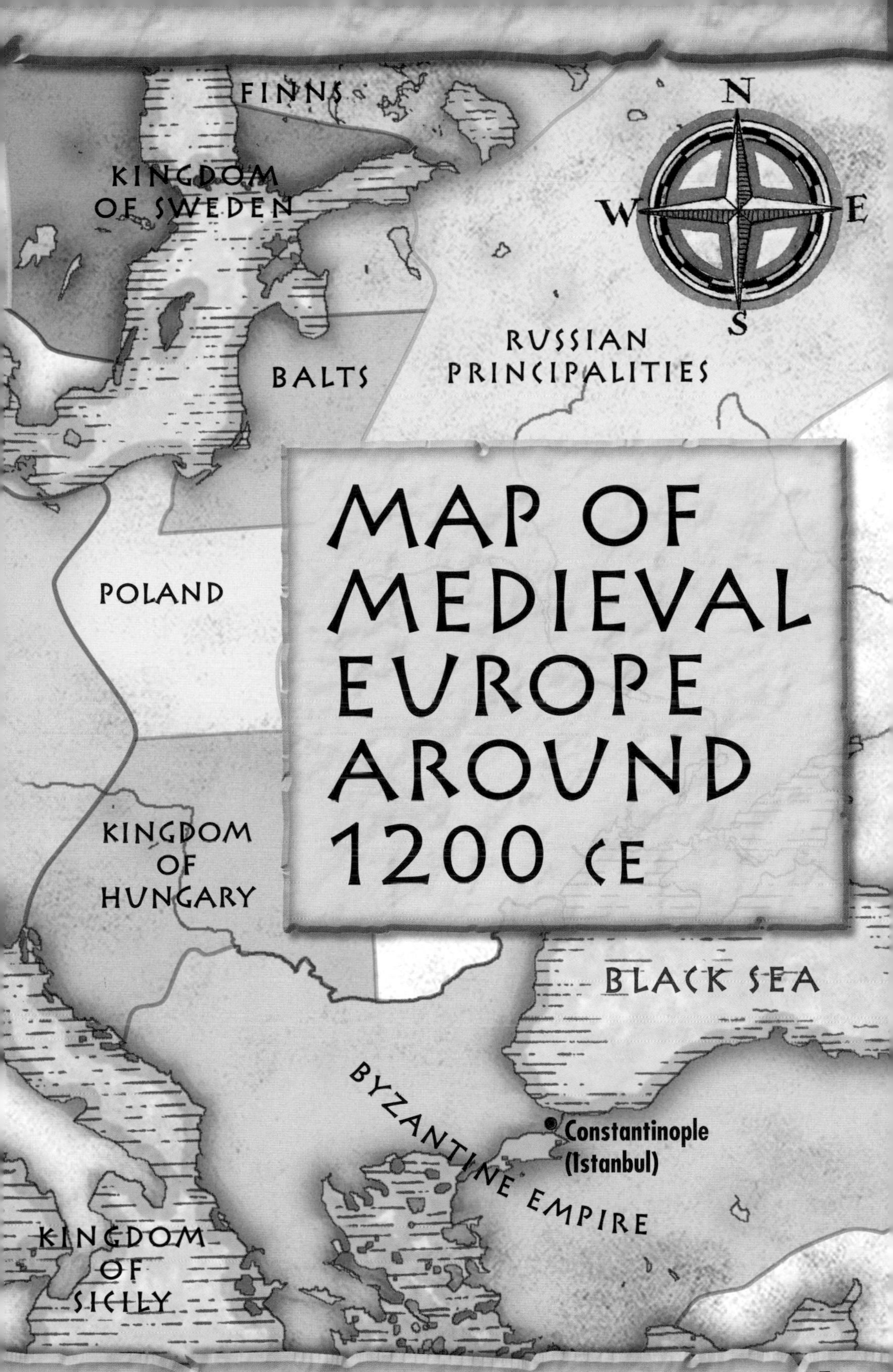
MAP OF MEDIEVAL EUROPE AROUND 1200 CE
FINNS
KINGDOM OF SWEDEN
BALTS
RUSSIAN PRINCIPALITIES
N
W
E
S
POLAND
KINGDOM OF HUNGARY
BLACK SEA
BYZANTINE EMPIRE
Constantinople (Istanbul)
KINGDOM OF SICILY

The 11th-century city walls of Avila, in Spain, are reinforced by turrets. Avila needs strong defenses because it is fought over by Christian and Muslim states.

CHAPTER 1

FACTS ABOUT MEDIEVAL EUROPE

If you want to see great castles and abbeys before they fall into ruins and discover if knights in shining armor really do rescue beautiful young women from dragons, then medieval Europe is the place for you. Experience the thrills of a tournament, the fun of a fair, and the devotion of a religious festival. But be careful—medieval Europe can be lawless, and disease is everywhere.

WHEN AND WHERE TO TRAVEL

The medieval period is the time between the fall of the Roman Empire in the 5th century CE and the **Renaissance** in the 15th century. This period is also known as the Middle Ages. The best time to visit medieval Europe is between 1100 and 1300.

THE EARLY MEDIEVAL PERIOD

The Roman Empire collapsed in the 5th century, after it was invaded by Germanic tribes. This threw Europe into chaos. Wars and invasions were happening everywhere. The economy was destroyed. Without trade to support them, many towns were abandoned.

Emperor Charlemagne (ruled 769–814 CE) is seen here in a 12th-century French stained-glass window. His empire included most of western Europe.

MEDIEVAL EUROPE AT ITS HEIGHT

By the early 12th century, things have started to improve in western Europe. Stable kingdoms with strong governments are able to enforce law and order and prevent invasions. New farming methods lead to greater prosperity, and towns begin to flourish again. If you arrive soon after 1100, you will find a society that is buzzing with new ideas. Europeans are at last feeling confident about the future. New schools and universities are being founded. Great cathedrals, monasteries, and castles are being built. Armies of **knights** are conquering new lands and expanding Europe's frontiers.

Wherever you travel in western Europe, the culture is very similar. From Norway to Italy, you will find the same styles of art and architecture, the same religious beliefs, the same political institutions, and even the same fashions. Educated people everywhere speak Latin, the language of the ancient Romans, as well as their own local language. If you want to see this splendid culture at its best, go to the kingdoms of France and England and to the German **Holy Roman Empire**.

THE END OF THE MEDIEVAL PERIOD

If you visit medieval Europe after 1300, you will find that **famine**, plague, peasant rebellions, and wars have left a lot of people miserable and suffering. In the 15th century the medieval period is drawing to a close as the Renaissance gradually transforms European civilization.

BEWARE OF THE BLACK DEATH!

Be especially careful to avoid the Black Death, a horrible plague that sweeps through Europe between 1346 and 1351. There are no effective treatments for the disease and, if you catch it, it will probably kill you.

GOOD AND BAD TIMES TO VISIT

793–911	The worst period for Viking pirate raids on western Europe
1066–1070	Stay away from England while it is being brutally conquered by the Normans
1096–1099	Crusading knights conquer the **Holy Land**
1100–1300	Medieval Europe is at the height of its prosperity
1337–1453	England and France fight the terrible Hundred Years' War
1346–1351	The Black Death kills about 25 million people in Europe

Key:

Stay away	Interesting times to visit	Best times to visit

CLIMATE AND LANDSCAPE

Along the Atlantic coasts you can expect rain at any time of year in medieval Europe. Take warm clothes even if you are visiting in the summer, since the weather can be cool. Winters here are usually not very cold. In central and eastern Europe the summers are warm and humid and the winters are freezing. Around the Mediterranean the summers are hot and dry and the winters are mild, with moderate rainfall. From about 1300 to 1800 the European climate turns colder than it is today.

FORESTS AND WILDLIFE

If you imagined that medieval Europe was going to have a wild landscape, think again. In most lowland areas, the forests were all cut down long ago to make way for fields and villages. The remaining woods are carefully managed to produce firewood and timber. However, you can still find bears, wolves, wild boar, and beavers in the densely forested mountains.

LEGENDARY WILDLIFE

Stories about heroes killing fire-breathing dragons are popular all over medieval Europe. Medieval people believe that dragons live in caves in remote, wild places. Dragons are thought to be evil, dangerous, greedy creatures that demand human sacrifices and hoard treasure. Fortunately, dragons are entirely imaginary!

THE FARMING LANDSCAPE

Most medieval Europeans are peasant farmers living in small villages of thatched cottages grouped around a church and the lord's **manor** house. In much of Europe, farms are very open, with few trees, hedges, or fences. Farmers use crop rotation to help keep the soil fertile. The village farmlands are divided into three great fields.

In this early 14th-century French illustration, a farmer uses oxen to plow a field. His wife follows, sowing seeds for next year's crops.

One of the fields is normally used to grow wheat. Another field is used to grow barley, oats, peas, or beans. The third is left **fallow** and used for livestock to graze. Dung from the animals helps fertilize the soil. The following year the field that was left fallow is used to grow grain. Meanwhile, the grain field is used for vegetables, and the vegetable field is left fallow to recover its fertility. Each great field is divided into strips.

WATERMILLS AND WINDMILLS

Watermills and windmills are a common sight in the countryside. They are used for making flour and powering pumps and other machinery. The *Domesday Book* (see page 59), written in 1087, lists 5,624 watermills in southern England alone.

THE CHURCH

The most important organization in medieval Europe is the church. Almost everyone you meet will be a Christian. The largest building in any community will usually be its church. Medieval Europeans are not tolerant of other religions, such as Judaism and Islam, which they believe are false. For your own safety, always show respect for Christian beliefs and to members of the clergy. If you do not, you might end up being burned as a heretic (see page 53).

RULERS OF THE CHURCH

The ruler of the church in western Europe is the **bishop** of Rome, who is also called the **pope**. Western Christians believe that the first pope was St. Peter, who became bishop of Rome around 60 CE. They believe that Jesus appointed St. Peter as the head of the Christian Church. Popes are elected by senior churchmen, called cardinals, who act as advisers to the pope.

This huge cathedral in York, in England, built between the 13th and 15th centuries, shows the wealth and power of the medieval church in England.

PATRON SAINTS

Patron saints are believed to protect places, people, or activities that were associated with the saints when they were alive. Here are some examples of patron saints who are well known in medieval times.

St. Christopher: Patron saint of travelers because he is believed to have carried the infant Jesus across a deep river.

St. Francis: Patron saint of animals because he loved nature and wildlife. He came from Assisi, in Italy, and founded the Franciscan order of friars in 1209.

St. Joseph: Patron saint of carpenters because he worked as a carpenter.

St. Lawrence: Patron saint of cooks because he was believed to have been executed by being roasted alive!

St. Nicholas: Patron saint of children because he is believed to have restored to life three young boys who had been murdered. He is better known today as Santa Claus.

St. Olaf: Patron saint of Norway. Olaf was a Norwegian king who was killed in 1030 for trying to convert his people to Christianity.

GOING TO CHURCH

People treat going to church on Sundays as a social occasion and always dress in their best clothes. The services are in Latin, a language most of the churchgoers do not understand. People also attend church for **baptisms** and funerals and to confess their sins to a priest. Weddings do not usually take place in church until the late medieval period.

PERSECUTION OF THE JEWS

After about 1000, Jews are increasingly persecuted. They are not permitted to own land and must wear distinctive clothing so they can always be identified. The church officially teaches tolerance of Jews, but most medieval Christians are hostile because the Bible says that Jews handed Jesus over to the Romans to be crucified. For this reason, Jews often face violent attacks.

NOBLES, KNIGHTS, AND SERFS

Medieval society is divided into different ranks. The highest rank is royalty. Then come the nobles or lords. The barons are the highest nobles. Below them are the knights. The middle ranks include merchants, craftsmen, and priests. At the lowest level are the serfs (peasant farmers). People are expected to know their place, so you should always show respect to those who appear to belong to a higher rank, even if they are rude to you.

BARONS AND KNIGHTS

Barons live in castles and have titles such as duke or count. Dukes are considered to have a higher rank than counts. Barons are responsible for providing knights for the king's army in wartime. They also keep law and order in the areas they govern on behalf of the king.

The lowest rank of nobles are the knights. Knights fight on horseback in the king's army.

This 13th-century illustration shows those who fight (knights and barons), those who pray (priests and monks), and those who work (everybody else)!

IT'S A MAN'S WORLD

Most medieval people are convinced that women are less intelligent than men. As a result, women are rarely allowed to hold positions of power and responsibility. Women also have fewer legal rights than men and can be beaten by their husbands if they are disobedient.

When they are not fighting, knights are managing their **estates** (lands). Most knights live in a large manor house in a village on their estate.

SERFS, NOT SLAVES

Serfs are peasant farmers who live on land owned by a lord. They are not allowed to leave their villages or marry without their lord's permission. A serf must give his lord one-third of all the crops he grows. He must also give one-tenth of his crops to support the church. This is called a tithe. Though serfs are not free, they are not slaves. The lord cannot take a serf away from his village and sell him. Serfs usually live in small cottages with walls of **wattle and daub** and thatched roofs.

RANK SPOTTING

The best way to tell people's rank is to look at their clothes. The more gorgeous and colorful their clothes are, the higher their rank. Barons are easy to spot because they will usually have a lot of servants and soldiers to show how important they are. Knights and merchants are the hardest to tell apart. Knights do not wear armor unless they are going into battle, since it is too heavy and uncomfortable. A successful merchant may be richer than many knights and wear finer clothes, but he is still considered to have a lower rank.

Serfs are shown harvesting wheat in this 13th-century German illumination. A good harvest is important for all ranks of medieval society.

THE KINGDOMS OF EUROPE

Most medieval European countries are ruled by kings, and the most influential countries are France, England, and the Holy Roman Empire.

KINGS

The church teaches that kings must always be obeyed because they are appointed by God. In reality, the power of medieval kings is limited by the nobles. As the king's leading subjects, nobles believe that they have a right to a say in the government of the kingdom. The most important task for a king is protecting his subjects. Kings must therefore be skilled at military tactics. Kings are also expected to pass good laws and enforce justice.

ENGLAND

Thanks to its strong monarchy, the kingdom of England is one of the best-governed countries in medieval Europe. Since it was conquered by the Duke of **Normandy**, William the Conqueror, in 1066, England has had a close but uneasy relationship with France. William replaced the old English aristocracy with his own supporters from Normandy in northern France. Since then, the upper classes in England have spoken French as their first language.

THE HUNDRED YEARS' WAR

Avoid France during the terrible Hundred Years' War with England (1337–1453). The war began when the English king Edward III claimed to be the rightful king of France. The fighting dragged on for 117 years. English armies won many battles, but they were eventually defeated and expelled from France.

FRANCE

France is the most important country in medieval Europe. French art, literature, music, and philosophy are admired all over Europe.

Until the reign of Philip Augustus (1179–1223), the French monarchy was weak. The French king could not control the French nobles, and the king of England often ruled more of France than the French monarch. By defeating England's King John and Holy Roman Emperor Otto IV in 1204, Philip made France the most powerful kingdom in Europe.

Philip Augustus, king of France (ruled 1180–1223), is shown talking to a bishop in this 14th-century illustration. The church teaches that kings get their power from God. ➤

THE HOLY ROMAN EMPIRE

The Holy Roman Empire was created by the German king Otto I (ruled 936–973) after he conquered much of what later became Italy, Germany, and other European territories. The Holy Roman emperors constantly have to struggle with the powerful German nobles and the rebellious cities of northern Italy. Despite this, the Holy Roman emperors claim to be successors to the ancient Roman emperors and say that they should have authority over the church. This last claim causes many damaging disputes with the popes.

OTHER IMPORTANT RULERS

Charlemagne, king of the Franks, ruled most of western Europe (ruled 769–814)
Alfred the Great, king of the English (ruled 871–899)
Frederick ("Redbeard") Barbarossa, Holy Roman emperor (ruled 1152–1190)
Louis IX, king of France (ruled 1226–1270)
Edward I, king of England (ruled 1272–1307)

FEUDALISM AND CHIVALRY

After the church, the most important influences on medieval society are **feudalism** and **chivalry**. Feudalism is a system in which a knight serves a lord or king in return for protection and support. Chivalry is a code of behavior followed by knights.

FEUDALISM

Feudalism began in the early medieval period as a way for kings and lords to keep armies of knights. Becoming a knight takes 14 years of training and a lot of money because armor, weapons, and a horse are very expensive. To afford all this, a knight must enter the service of a rich lord or king. The knight has to become a vassal (legal dependant) by swearing an oath of loyalty to the lord.

OATHS

An oath is a solemn promise made in front of witnesses and a Bible or other holy object. An oath is used when making important agreements. Breaking an oath is considered a great sin and can be punished with loss of lands or even death. The church teaches that oath breakers will be sent to hell after they die. This late 14th-century French illustration shows a knight, with his hand on a Bible, swearing an oath of loyalty to his king.

Both the knight and the lord have duties toward each other. The knight must fight for his lord in wartime and give him political support. In return, the lord promises to protect the knight. The lord also gives the knight an estate so that he can support himself. This estate is called a **fief**. If a knight is disloyal, he can lose his fief. A knight is free to seek a new lord if his lord does not protect or support him.

CHIVALRY

Chivalry is a code of conduct for knights on and off the battlefield. A chivalrous knight must be a good horseman and be skilled in using weapons. He should show mercy to wounded knights and those who wish to surrender. He is also expected to be loyal to his feudal lord and be a good Christian. One of the best ways for a knight to prove this is to go on a **crusade** (Christian war). Knights must be courteous toward women, protect the weak, and be generous to the sick and poor. Unfortunately, knights do not always live up to these ideals.

LET'S TALK

All medieval kings rule with the advice of a council made up of barons and senior churchmen. In the 1200s King Henry III of England also begins to consult knights, merchants, and other important people. This larger council becomes the first parliament. *Parliament* comes from the French word *parlement*, meaning "a talk."

Kings issued charters (legal documents) to grant or confirm the legal rights of their subjects. This charter was issued by King John of England (ruled 1199–1216).

MEDIEVAL EDUCATION

Medieval education is run by the church. There are cathedral schools and some exciting new institutions called universities. Schools and universities exist mainly to educate boys who wish to become priests. However, more and more young boys are being sent to universities because it will help them have careers in government, law, and medicine.

MEDIEVAL UNIVERSITIES

If you are interested in ideas and arguments, you should definitely visit some European universities in the late 1100s. At this time, new ideas from the Islamic world and the rediscovery of lost works by the ancient Greek philosophers Plato and Aristotle are causing great excitement—and plenty of arguments. Some see these new ideas as a threat to Christian beliefs. Others see them as a way to gain a better understanding of the Bible. The oldest university is in Bologna, in Italy, and was founded in 1088. The largest is in Paris and was founded around 1150.

STUDENT LIFE

Teaching in a medieval cathedral school is not done in a classroom. The teacher will just gather his class in a quiet place in the cathedral and give a lecture. The lecture is followed by a discussion. Students practice writing using a **stylus** on wax-covered tablets, but these are not suitable for note-taking in lectures, so students have to remember what they hear.

AN UNFAIR SYSTEM

If you want to try medieval education for yourself, just go along and sit in on a lesson or lecture. You will be expected to pay the teacher, though. Poor people cannot afford this, so most do not even learn to read and write. Only boys can go to school and university. Girls from noble families are sometimes educated at home by private tutors.

The exams are tough question- and-answer sessions in front of a panel of teachers. Most university students

This 14th-century French illustration shows a university teacher lecturing to students.

are between 14 and 18 years old. They have a bad reputation for getting drunk, singing rude songs, and chasing girls. Fights between students and townsfolk are common.

THE MEDIEVAL CURRICULUM

The first stage of medieval university education covers three subjects: grammar, rhetoric (public speaking), and dialectic (logic). This is supposed to teach students to think and express themselves clearly. The second stage includes four subjects: arithmetic, geometry, astronomy, and music. When a student has completed both stages, he is given a degree.

WHAT TO WEAR

Most medieval people view travelers with a mixture of curiosity and suspicion. Travelers may bring news of great events, stories about faraway lands, and have exotic things to sell. But they may also be spies in disguise, and they may spread disease. If sickness breaks out just after you have arrived in town, watch out. If the locals think it is your fault, you could be attacked. Because of this, it is best to wear the same clothes as everyone else so as not to draw attention to yourself.

MEDIEVAL FASHION

If you are visiting between 1100 and 1300, make sure you take a tunic. This should reach the ground if you are a woman or the calves if you are a man. Women wear close-fitting tunics to show off their figures, but men's are cut loose for freedom of movement when riding or working. In public, married women should cover their hair with a hat or veil. The rich wear clothes made of silk, velvet, satin, fur, and linen. The common folk do their best to imitate the dress of the upper classes, but can usually only afford woolen cloth. Children's clothes are just miniature versions of the clothes worn by adults.

veil

circlet

long tunic

girdle

This illustration shows the clothes worn by a typical well-to-do medieval European woman in the 12th century.

WARNING: DANGEROUS SHOES

Shoes with pointed toes are worn by men and women in medieval times. After 1300 men's pointy shoes start getting longer and longer. By 1400 they are so long they have to be tied back to the wearer's knees to stop him from tripping over them! The leather shoes shown here date from the 13th and 14th centuries.

HAIRSTYLES

If you are a man, grow your hair to about shoulder length. There is no need to grow a beard, since many men prefer to be clean-shaven. Women and girls should grow their hair long. If you cannot do this, wear a hairpiece. Do not worry if you get found out—medieval women cheat, too! Women usually part their hair in the middle and arrange it in long braids. Until 1150 the braids are worn loose. After that, they are coiled around the head or over the ears and held in place with nets.

STAY OUT OF THE SUN!

Modern tourists like to get a good suntan when they go on vacation. In medieval Europe you will get more respect by staying pale. Upper-class women are very careful about protecting their skin from the sun whenever they go out. Having white skin is a status symbol because it shows everyone that you do not have to work outside for a living. If they want to add a bit of color to their cheeks, women just dab on a rosy-red mixture of flour and beetroot juice.

Melrose Abbey, in Scotland, was originally built in the 12th century and then rebuilt in the 15th century.

CHAPTER 2

WHERE TO GO AND WHAT TO DO

There is no shortage of things to do and see in medieval Europe. All the top attractions—the great cathedrals, monasteries, and castles—welcome visitors. Even better, most public entertainments, such as tournaments and plays, are free. You can enjoy a unique shopping experience in the carnival atmosphere of a fair or just browse among the many food and craft stores in a thriving town. But watch where you put your feet: medieval towns are not the cleanest places.

MEDIEVAL TOWNS

"Town air brings freedom." This German saying explains the appeal of medieval town life. Many people in the country are serfs (peasant farmers) who have to obey their lord. But townsfolk are free. Whether they are rich or poor, they can travel, seek whatever employment they wish, and marry without having to ask the permission of a lord. As a result, there is a buzz in the towns that you will not find in the countryside. But there is a downside, too. Because there are no sewers or trash collections, medieval towns are dirty, stinky, and full of rats. These unhygienic conditions mean that diseases such as the plague spread more quickly in the towns than the countryside. Also, if you do not want to spend a cold night outdoors, make sure you arrive at a town before dark. Town gates are locked at night to keep out robbers.

↖ In this 14th-century painting, the streets of the Italian city of Siena are crowded with people shopping and meeting friends.

SIGHTSEEING

You will probably want to head for the cathedral first. This will usually be the biggest and most spectacular building. Large towns often have many other beautiful churches worth visiting. All the important towns have defensive walls, which you can walk along in peacetime, with impressive gatehouses. There are also some magnificent **secular** buildings, such as palaces, guildhalls, and market halls. Outdoor markets are great for shopping and takeout food. After walking around all those dirty streets, you can finish your day with a visit to a public bathhouse. Yes, medieval people really do take baths—but not every day!

GUILDS

The most influential organizations in towns are the guilds. Guilds are associations of merchants and craftsmen. These set standards for training and for the quality of products. Entry to guilds is tightly controlled. Parents pay a master-craftsman to train one of their

NIGHTLIFE

Since there is no source of artificial light other than candles and burning torches, many people will not go out at night for fear of being robbed on the unlit streets. Also, most entertainments, such as plays and tournaments, take place during the daytime.

children as an **apprentice**. Training starts at the age of 11 and lasts for seven years. Apprentices are not paid during this time. After he has finished his training, an apprentice becomes a **journeyman**, working for wages. Only after he has completed a top-quality test piece is a journeyman admitted to the guild as a master-craftsman.

ARCHITECTURE

You will notice that the great cathedrals, churches, and monasteries of medieval Europe are built in two easily recognized architectural styles: Romanesque and Gothic. Romanesque is the older of the two styles and is fashionable from around 800 to 1150. In England, Romanesque is usually called Norman architecture. This is because it only became widespread in England after the Norman Conquest in 1066. The Gothic style started in France in the 1140s and spread to all of western Europe by 1200. It remains popular until the end of the medieval period.

St. Kilian Cathedral, completed in 1188, is the fourth-largest Romanesque church in modern-day Germany.

SOME GREAT CATHEDRALS TO VISIT

Place	Date begun	Style
Pisa, Italy	1063	Romanesque
Santiago de Compostela, Spain	1075	Romanesque
Durham, England	1093	Romanesque
Nôtre Dame, Paris, France	1163	Gothic
Canterbury, England	1175	Gothic
Chartres, France	1194	Gothic
Cologne, Germany	1248	Gothic

ROMANESQUE ARCHITECTURE

Romanesque architecture is heavy and solid. The buildings have very thick pillars and walls to support their heavy stone barrel **vault** roofs. All the arches and windows have round tops, and the arches are often decorated with a jagged dog-tooth pattern.

GOTHIC ARCHITECTURE

You will recognize Gothic architecture (see pages 24–25) because of its pointed arches and the diagonal rib vaults used in the roofs. Gothic buildings are taller and more graceful than Romanesque ones. Their large windows mean that Gothic buildings are full of light inside, and their high vaulted roofs seem to soar upward. On the outside of many Gothic cathedrals you can see spectacular arches called flying buttresses. These are used to transfer the weight of the roof to the ground without the need for thick walls.

INSIDE A MEDIEVAL CHURCH

Medieval churches and cathedrals are colorful and richly decorated inside. The windows are filled with colored glass. The walls are whitewashed and covered with paintings of scenes from Bible stories or from the lives of popular saints. Because most people are unable to read, the paintings teach them about Christian beliefs.

VISITING A MONASTERY

Monasteries are communities of monks led by an **abbot**. Monks spend much of their time praying. They pray to God to save their own souls and also to save the souls of people who have given land or money to the monastery. A monastery includes a church, a cloister where monks can exercise in bad weather, a dormitory where the monks sleep, a refectory where they eat together, an infirmary for sick monks, and many other buildings such as toilet blocks, stores, kitchens, and guest rooms. The abbot usually has a separate house. Through donations, monasteries have built up very big estates, and many have become very wealthy.

A MONK'S LIFE

In addition to praying, monks must work (either on the monastery's lands or by copying books) and spend time studying the Bible. Monks must live simply and cannot own any personal belongings or get married. Monks must always obey their abbot, and once they have entered a monastery they must stay there for life. Monks are instantly recognizable because their hair is cut in a **tonsure** (shaved on top).

Most medieval monasteries have cloisters like these, where monks can enjoy walking.

VISITING ARRANGEMENTS

Monasteries are surrounded by walls, so all visitors must report to the gatehouse. Though there are no entry fees, it will be appreciated if you make a donation to the monastery. All monasteries have guest rooms for visitors who want to stay overnight. Churchmen and **pilgrims** can stay for free, but other visitors may have to pay. Guests are treated with great respect. Monks must bow their heads and kneel on the ground when greeting a guest. They will even wash your feet as a sign of humility.

These monks, from a 13th-century manuscript, are singing psalms during a church service. ➞

NUNS

Women who devote their lives to God are called nuns. They live in nunneries that are led by an **abbess**. Because they are women, nuns have a lower status than monks. Nunneries do not attract as many donations as monasteries, so they are smaller and poorer.

FRIARS

Friars live a simple religious life like monks, but they do not live in monasteries. Friars spend their time preaching and teaching among the common people, especially in towns. Do not be offended if a friar asks you for food or money. Friars are supposed to live by begging.

CASTLES

Castles are an important part of medieval life. They are first built in France in the 10th century and are being built all over Europe by the end of the 11th century. A castle is not just a fortress. It is also the home of a baron and a center for local government. The age of castle building comes to an end in late medieval times with the development of cannons, which can easily batter down a castle's high stone walls.

keep

workshops and stables

ward

WHAT IS IN A CASTLE?

At the heart of a typical castle is a massive square stone tower called a keep. This contains the living quarters for the lord, his family, household knights, and servants, together with a great hall for entertaining, stores, an armory, kitchens, and a chapel. Surrounding the keep is a long stone wall reinforced with towers and a strong gatehouse. The space between the keep and the outer wall is called the ward. This contains workshops and stables.

VISITING ARRANGEMENTS

Castles are designed to be hard to get into, but that is only in wartime. Because castles are homes and administrative centers, there needs to be access during the day for family members, soldiers, friends, servants, and people coming to do business. If you are a respectable visitor, you will usually be made welcome.

CASTLE DEFENSES

Castles are strong enough to withstand a siege for months or even years. To make it harder for enemies to get in, a castle is usually surrounded with a flooded moat or built on a hilltop. Moats are crossed by a drawbridge, which can be lifted up in wartime.

gatehouse

drawbridge

moat

This is an illustration of a late 12th-century castle. The keep, in the center, contains the living quarters.

ENTERTAINMENT

There are no televisions, radios, or computer games in medieval Europe, but there is plenty of live entertainment. You can join in rough sports, such as medieval versions of soccer and hockey, play quiet board games such as chess, watch a play, go to a dance, or listen to a **minstrel** singing. Men can visit a tavern, but respectable ladies will stay at home and practice their needlework.

THRILLS AND SPILLS

If you want to see the exciting spectacle of knights in action, go and watch a tournament. Tournaments begin with **jousts**, where two knights charge at one another with lances (spears) and try to get their opponent off his horse. The main event is the **melee**, a mock battle fought between two groups of knights. Though the swords and spears are blunted, melees are very rough, and injuries and even deaths are common.

In this 14th-century illustration some ladies watch two knights jousting at a tournament in France.

Despite the risks, tournaments are popular with young knights. Those who are successful, such as the English knight William Marshal (1147–1219), can become very rich by winning horses and armor from their opponents.

MYSTERY PLAYS

Medieval drama always has a religious or moral purpose, but that does not mean it is dull. Most actors are amateurs, and everyone in the local community joins in, not just by acting but also by playing music or making stage scenery and colorful costumes. Even audiences can get involved in the action during a play. People get most enthusiastic about mystery plays. These are always based on Bible stories. Mystery plays are organized by craft guilds and are performed at religious festivals. Morality plays are also popular. Humor is used to get the message across, so they can be very funny. If you visit before 1200 you will find that most plays are performed in churches. After that date the scenery becomes more spectacular and performances are held outside on temporary stages built in churchyards or marketplaces, or even on wagons.

TRAVELING ENTERTAINERS

It always causes excitement when a band of traveling entertainers (jongleurs) arrives in town. Jongleurs include acrobats, dancers, jugglers, magicians, and minstrels. Minstrels are poets and musicians who sing romantic songs about chivalry and love. Many of these songs were originally composed by troubadours (poets from the noble families of southern France).

THE SPORT OF KINGS

The favorite pastime of the upper classes is hunting deer and wild boar on horseback with dogs. They also enjoy hunting wild fowl with specially trained falcons. Do not even think about hunting without permission. Poaching is severely punished everywhere, especially in England. Here, William the Conqueror (ruled 1066–1087) introduced the death penalty for anyone who killed the king's deer illegally.

SHOPPING

Shopaholics will enjoy medieval Europe. Stores open at dawn and stay open until nightfall. Ask locally about Sunday trading. Medieval Europeans do not strictly enforce Sunday as a rest day, even though most of them are devout Christians. Markets are held outdoors once a week. The main shopping streets lead off from the market square. Stores selling similar goods are grouped together. In one street you will find only butchers, in another weavers, and so on. Market days are very busy. Few people live more than a day's walk from a town, so it is quite easy for country folk to visit markets to sell farm produce and to buy cloth, pottery, and other goods.

FUN AT THE FAIR

The shopping event of the year is the annual fair, which lasts several days. Traders from all over Europe come to sell woolen cloth, linen, Chinese silk, metalwork, pottery, foodstuffs, exotic spices, and much more. Fairs also attract traveling entertainers, so there is a real carnival atmosphere. The best fairs are in Champagne, in France. Its location, halfway between the Mediterranean and the North Sea, makes Champagne an important trading area. Whichever time of year you visit, you should be able to find a town that is holding a fair.

This Italian illustration, dated around 1400, shows master craftsmen making patterned tapestries on wooden frames.

WHAT TO BUY

- **Aquamanile**: One of these bronze jugs, made in the shape of a knight on horseback, will make a great ornament.
- **Chess set**: Chess is a popular game in the Middle Ages, and you can get some lovely ivory chess sets carved from the tusks of African elephants or walruses from the Arctic Ocean. The carved ivory knight in the picture is from a 13th-century chess set.
- **Cloth-of-gold**: This is fantastically expensive cloth embroidered with real gold thread.
- **Souvenir badges**: These are sold at all important shrines and pilgrim centers. They are usually made of lead and are nailed on to walking poles.

MEDIEVAL MONEY

The most common medieval coin is the silver denier, or penny. People make small change by cutting pennies up into halves and quarters. Coins are not dated, but they carry the name and portrait of the ruler who has issued them. If traveling from one kingdom to another, you can change your money at a moneychanger's shop. Do not worry too much if you cannot find one: a coin is always worth its weight in silver. But do watch out for clipped coins. Someone has sneakily trimmed some silver off the edges of these, so they are not worth as much as unclipped coins. In England, people who are found guilty of clipping coins will have their right hand cut off.

This painting, dated 1407, shows Pope Alexander III (center, riding) and Holy Roman Emperor Frederick Barbarossa (center, walking) entering Rome.

CHAPTER 3

ON THE MOVE

Travel in medieval Europe can be slow and uncomfortable, so relax and take it easy. If you travel in short stages, you can take the opportunity to meet many fascinating travelers and listen to the tales they have to tell. There is no shortage of accommodation for travelers and, if you are lucky, you might even be invited to stay in a castle for the night. But be careful as well. Not everyone you meet on the road will be friendly.

ROADS AND WATERWAYS

Summer is the best time of year to travel in medieval Europe. There is less of a chance of storms if you are traveling by sea, and the roads will be at their driest. In wet weather, horses and carts churn them up into horrible mud baths.

MEDIEVAL TRAVELERS

Most of the people you will meet on the road will be peasants, **tinkers**, merchants, or entertainers traveling to the nearest market town. You will also see lords and knights on their way to **court** or to join the king's army for a military campaign. Even kings travel a lot, visiting their estates and going hunting. You may also meet pilgrims on their way to Rome in Italy or Santiago de Compostela in Spain (see page 46).

ON THE ROAD

The fastest way to travel overland is on horseback. Horses are expensive to buy, but it is also possible to rent them. Most people have to walk. The most common vehicles are two-wheeled carts, pulled by oxen or horses. These are used to transport goods rather than people. If you have more money, you can travel in a carriage. But they bump and lurch all over the road. Take some cushions with you if you travel this way.

This illustration of a horse-drawn cart was made about 1340.

OVER THE SEA

In early medieval times, most ships are just big open boats, such as Viking longships. If the weather is bad, you get wet and cold. The most common types of ship used from 1100 to 1300 are the **hulk** and the smaller **cog**. Both types of ship are built to be broad and sturdy so they can carry large cargoes and have a single mast with a broad square sail. By 1200, if used as warships, they have wooden "castles" built on the bow and stern. Traveling by ship is still not very comfortable, but at least you can sleep and take shelter below deck in bad weather. Expect awful food. When at sea, sailors mainly eat hard **ship's biscuit** and meat or fish that has been salted to preserve it.

This 14th-century illustration shows two trade ships struggling in a high wind. An oared galley (warship) can be seen in the background.

FOOD AND DRINK

You will have to do without some of your favorite foods and drinks while you are visiting medieval Europe. There are no chocolates, bananas, corn, tomatoes, chilis, teas, coffees, or even potatoes! All these foods are still unknown. You will not be offered much sweet food, either. Honey is a treat, and sugar is a very expensive luxury that is imported from the Middle East. Only wealthy people can afford to have a sweet tooth.

RICH AND POOR

If you are traveling on a tight budget, expect a diet of wholemeal bread, butter, and cheese, or gruel (made of barley, dried peas, and seasonal vegetables) for breakfast, dinner, lunch, and supper. Dinner (served at around 11 A.M.) and supper (served at around 6 P.M.) are the main meals of the day. Breakfast, served at daybreak, and lunch, served between dinner and supper, are light meals and are usually eaten only by working people.

This part of the 11th-century Bayeux tapestry shows a bishop blessing the food at the start of a feast.

Your best chance of getting fresh meat will be in the fall, when young animals that cannot be fed through the winter are slaughtered. If you have more money, you can vary your diet with soft white bread, spiced food, pies, desserts, and lots of roast and boiled meat. On some days your choice of food will be limited for religious reasons. Because the Bible says that Jesus was crucified on a Friday, meat eating is banned on that day of the week (though fish is allowed). **Lent** is a season of religious fasting, during which meat, eggs, and dairy products are banned.

SPICE OF LIFE

Medieval people like strongly flavored food. Spices such as pepper, cloves, nutmeg, and ginger are popular for flavoring both meat and fruit dishes, but they are very expensive because they have to be imported from India and Indonesia. Home-grown herbs, such as thyme, sage, mustard, and garlic, are also widely used.

DON'T DRINK THE WATER

Finding safe drinking water in medieval Europe is a problem. Medieval people know that drinking water is a shortcut to a stomachache, so they avoid it if they can. Instead, in northern Europe everyone drinks beer—1 gallon (around 4 liters) of it every day. Fortunately, medieval beer is very low in alcohol. In southern Europe, wine is the most common drink. Like beer, medieval wine contains much less alcohol than modern wine.

WHERE TO STAY

Medieval Europe has plenty of places for travelers to stay. Towns have lots of inns, and many private houses will provide you with "bed and breakfast." The church also has hostels, and most monasteries have comfortable guest rooms. If you look like a respectable and well-to-do traveler, you might even be invited to stay in a castle or palace.

In this 14th-century Italian painting, a thirsty traveler is offered a drink as he arrives at an inn.

ROOM AT THE INN

Medieval inns are built around courtyards, with gates that can be locked at night to guard against thieves. Around the courtyard there are stables for travelers' horses. The travelers themselves stay in rooms above the stables. Inns provide meals and drinks. Most towns have rules about the quality of beer and food in order to make sure that travelers are not cheated. Many inns have entertainment, and guests can play board games. Gambling is also common, but it is best not to get involved because there are many cheats, some of whom use **loaded dice**, for example.

IN AN EMERGENCY

If you are really down on your luck, remember that monasteries have a duty to give free food to the poor. It is also worth hanging around castle kitchens. Feeding the poor is a Christian duty, so the rich have more food cooked than they and their guests can possibly eat. This means there are plenty of leftovers to be given away.

In this kitchen scene from the "Lutrell Psalter," a cook is preparing roast fowls and servants are carrying dishes out to the hall for the guests.

LIVING IT UP

Do not be afraid to ask if you can stay the night at a castle. Giving lavish hospitality is an easy way for rich people to show off, so they like having guests. Best of all, it will not cost you a penny. Do not expect great luxury, though. Castles and great houses are drafty and cold in winter and there is little privacy. Often it will only be the owner and his wife who have a private bedroom. Dinner in the great hall is the high point of the stay. You will be invited to eat and drink your fill at tables laden with soups, pastries, meats, and puddings. Resident singers and minstrels may provide music while you eat. After dinner you can go to bed—on the floor of the hall with everybody else! You will not have a mattress here, but the floor will be covered with rush mats or straw.

BEAT THE BUGS

With the poor standards of hygiene in medieval Europe, you are bound to wake up one morning covered with little red bite marks. That grubby straw-filled mattress you slept on was full of bedbugs! Bedbugs do not carry serious diseases, but those bites will itch, and if you scratch them they could get infected. Keep the bugs away by going to bed with bunches of strong-smelling mint.

PILGRIMAGE

Many of the travelers you meet on the road will be on pilgrimages to holy sites. Pilgrimages are long journeys made for religious reasons—for example, to show devotion to God or a popular saint. Pilgrims hope that by showing their devotion in this way they will get into heaven more easily or perhaps be cured of a disease. People are often ordered to go on a pilgrimage by the church as a way for them to earn God's forgiveness for sins they have committed in their daily lives.

TOP PILGRIMAGE DESTINATIONS

Canterbury: England's top pilgrimage spot is the tomb of the murdered archbishop of Canterbury, St. Thomas Beckett.

Santiago de Compostela, Spain: Crowds of pilgrims flock here to visit the tomb of the disciple St. James (Santiago).

Rome, Italy: Not only is Rome the headquarters of the pope, but pilgrims can also visit the **catacombs** containing the bodies of hundreds of early Christian **martyrs**.

The Holy Land: Visiting the land where Jesus lived and died is the ultimate pilgrimage. It is also the most dangerous because the Holy Land is a battle zone between Christians and Muslims.

ON THE ROAD WITH THE PILGRIMS

Short pilgrimages to a local shrine have a vacation atmosphere to them, but a long pilgrimage can involve many months of hardship. Pilgrims are not supposed to take money or valuables with them. This is to help protect them against robbers. In fact, most pilgrims do take money so that they can buy souvenirs and treats, but it is not really necessary. There are church hostels along the main pilgrimage routes where pilgrims can spend the night and get a simple meal for free. Pilgrims often travel in groups for safety and company, telling stories (see page 59) and singing to pass the time. They stop to pray at the wayside shrines that you will see along pilgrim routes.

THE CRUSADES

A crusade is the name given to a holy war to defend the Christian religion. Crusaders see themselves as armed pilgrims and believe they will go straight to heaven if they die in the fight. Most crusades are led by knights, barons, or kings. The most famous crusading kings are Richard I of England ("the Lionheart") and Louis IX of France ("St. Louis").

The first crusade was called in 1095 by Pope Urban II to capture Jerusalem from the Muslims. Seven more crusades were called to defend the Holy Land against Muslim counterattack. In 1291, after many years of bloodshed, the Muslims drove the crusaders out of the Holy Land for good.

This French illustration, dated around 1400, shows the loss of Jerusalem to the Muslim leader Saladin in 1187. The defeat was a great blow to the crusaders. ⇗

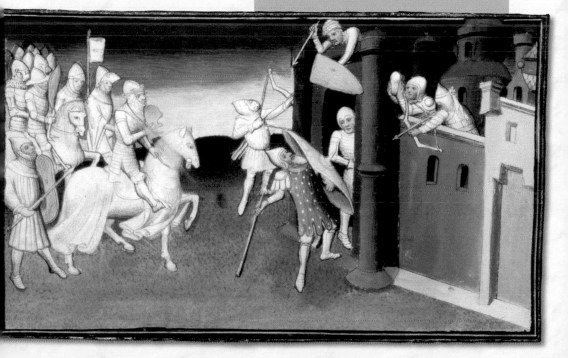

The Heiliggeist Hospital in Nuremberg, in modern-day Germany, was founded in 1331 and later extended.

CHAPTER 4

TAKING CARE OF YOURSELF

Do not travel alone in medieval Europe. Lone travelers are easy prey for robbers, and if you become sick it is good to have a friend to take care of you. Protecting yourself against disease will be especially difficult. Medieval people have a very poor understanding of the causes of disease, and most food is prepared in conditions we would think of as very unhygienic. And do not commit any crimes—medieval punishments are extremely unpleasant!

DISEASE AND MEDICAL CARE

The greatest danger for the traveler in medieval Europe is disease. Infectious diseases flourish in the unhygienic towns and villages, and food poisoning is a constant danger. Unfortunately, visiting a doctor (if you can find one) will probably only make things worse. Seeking out a "wise woman" or herbalist is safer. Even if her remedy does not work, it probably will not seriously harm you.

A STRANGE APPROACH TO MEDICINE

Medieval doctors base their understanding of disease on ideas handed down by the ancient Greeks. The Greeks believed that the human body is made up of four **humors**: blood, choler, phlegm, and melancholy. If someone gets sick, medieval people think they have too much or too little of a particular humor. Generally, doctors try to balance the humors by suggesting certain foods and drinks. But if a patient has a fever, doctors may think that the patient has too much blood and is overheating. They may try to cure the patient by bleeding to remove the excess blood. This, of course, just weakens the patient and increases the chance of death. Doctors bleed patients by cutting a vein or by using slimy, blood-sucking leeches. Yuck!

DENTAL TREATMENT

If you get a toothache, you will need to find a barber. He will pull out the aching tooth. But there are no anesthetics to dull the pain. Fortunately, because they do not have a lot of sugar in their diet, medieval people do not suffer from tooth decay as much as we do.

HOSPITALS

Most medieval towns have at least one hospital. Big cities such as Florence, Paris, or London have several. Hospitals are run by the church because caring for the sick is a Christian duty. Hospitals provide little more than basic nursing care and a priest to comfort the dying. Patients often have to share beds.

LEPERS

The disease that frightens medieval people most is not the plague but rather leprosy. Leprosy is a skin disease that causes horrible disfigurement. Lepers are forced to live in isolated hospitals and must carry a bell to warn people of their approach. Helping a leper is seen as a holy act because most people are scared to go anywhere near them. In fact, leprosy is not easy to catch, so there is no need to panic if you are approached by a leper.

In this 15th-century illustration, a doctor helps a bedridden patient. Meanwhile, the patient's wife is visiting an apothecary's shop to buy medicine.

LIFE EXPECTANCY

You will quickly notice that there are not many elderly people in medieval Europe. (Only 5 percent of medieval Europeans live to their seventies.) But the early years are the most dangerous. Over 25 percent of all children die before the age of five, and only half survive to adulthood. Around 20 percent of adult women die during childbirth.

CRIME AND PUNISHMENT

No one in medieval Europe keeps reliable records of crimes, but all the evidence suggests that violent crime is common. With no banks and only primitive locks on heavy wooden strongboxes, it is difficult to keep your belongings safe. Medieval people often bury their valuables for safekeeping. When traveling, do as medieval folk do and join a band of other travelers for protection against robbers.

LAW ENFORCEMENT

There are no police forces in medieval Europe. In England, investigating crime is the responsibility of royal officials, such as the county sheriffs. Offenders usually have to pay a fine or pay compensation to the victim. Murderers, and thieves who are caught red-handed, are hanged. Prisons are used mainly to hold people awaiting trial or execution, rather than as a form of punishment. Castle basements are favorite places for prisons. They are gloomy, damp, unhealthy, and very hard to escape from.

Medieval prisons are uncomfortable and unhygienic places, but most prisoners are in no hurry to leave, since they are simply being held there while awaiting their execution.

Suspected criminals who fail to appear in court when summoned can be named as outlaws. Anyone is allowed to kill an outlaw without fear of punishment. In England, the worst punishment (used for traitors) is hanging, drawing, and quartering. The victim is hanged until half dead. Then, he is disembowelled (drawing).

Finally, he is beheaded and cut into four pieces (quartering). The remains of traitors are displayed in public places as a warning to others.

Hanging is the most common form of execution. Only nobles are given the privilege of a quick death by being beheaded.

ROBIN HOOD

The most famous English medieval outlaw is Robin Hood. He became a popular hero because he is supposed to have robbed the rich to give to the poor. No one is quite sure when Robin lived. Many of the stories about him are set during the reign of King Richard I (1189–1199), but most historians think he lived over a hundred years later.

RELIGIOUS CRIME

Visitors to medieval Europe should not argue about religion with strangers. Disagreeing with the teaching of the church is a crime called heresy. If you are suspected of heresy in France, Spain, or Italy, you can be arrested and handed over to the **Holy Inquisition** for questioning. This could really spoil your trip because the Inquisition is allowed to torture suspects if it thinks they are not telling the truth.

WITCHCRAFT

Belief in witches is common in medieval Europe. Witchcraft is illegal and can be punished by burning. However, the church teaches that most witches are frauds and do not really have magical powers, so executions are rare. It is not until the 16th century that Europeans become really afraid of witchcraft.

These stone carvings of angels and saints are from a decorated doorway in the medieval cathedral of Nôtre Dame, in Paris.

CHAPTER 5

USEFUL INFORMATION

You will enjoy your visit to medieval Europe a lot more if you know a bit about the history of the period. Many sources of information about the medieval period have survived to the present day. These tell us not only what happened, but also what people thought about their own lives. There are also records of the languages that people spoke during medieval times. Knowing something about these will help you make friends during your travels.

LANGUAGE

The best language to learn before visiting medieval Europe is Latin, the language of the ancient Romans. After the fall of the Roman Empire, Latin fell out of use as an everyday language, but it continued to be used as the language of the church. All the holy scriptures were translated into Latin and all church business was conducted in Latin. Few people outside the church could read and write in the early medieval period. Kings therefore employed churchmen as administrators, so Latin became the language of government, too. Because they could all speak and write to one another in Latin, it was easy for educated people to travel around Europe. Even the smallest village had a priest who knew Latin.

NATIONAL LANGUAGES

The languages of modern Europe developed in medieval times. Most of the languages of western Europe belong to two families. The Romance family of languages includes Italian, French, Spanish, and Portuguese. These languages developed from local dialects of Latin spoken in late Roman times. The second family of languages includes German, Dutch, English, Danish, Swedish, and Norwegian. These languages developed from languages spoken by ancient Germanic tribes.

MEDIEVAL ENGLISH

English speakers who think they will have an easy time visiting medieval England will be in for a shock. The English language did not gain its modern pronunciation and spelling until around 1600. Medieval English actually sounded very different from modern English. The meaning of the words is not so difficult to figure out, but it will probably take you a while to get used to it. The medieval English people whom you meet will probably think you talk a bit strangely, too.

USEFUL MEDIEVAL ENGLISH WORDS

Modern English	Medieval English	Latin
food	*fode*	*cibus*
water	*water*	*aqua*
bread	*breed*	*panis*
milk	*melk*	*lac*
soup	*potage*	*ius*
father	*fader*	*pater*
mother	*moder*	*mater*
daughter	*doghter*	*filia*
son	*sone*	*filius*

The following passage, describing a knight, is taken from medieval poet Geoffrey Chaucer's *Canterbury Tales*:

A knyght there was, and that a worthy man,
That fro the tyme that he first began
To ridden out, he loved chivalrie,
Trouthe and honour, freedom and curteisie.
Ful worthy was he in his lordes werre,
And therto hadde he ridden, no man ferre,
As wel in cristendom as in hethenesse,
And evere honoured for his worthynesse. [. . .]
He was a verray, parfit gentil knight.

There was a knight, and he was a distinguished man,
That from the time that he first began
To go on campaigns, had loved chivalry,
Truth and honor, freedom and courtesy.
He had served bravely in his lord's wars,
And no man had traveled so far on campaign as he had,
Both in Christian lands and heathen ones too,
And he was always honored for his good character. [. . .]
He was a true, perfect, noble knight.

HOW DO WE KNOW ABOUT MEDIEVAL EUROPE?

We know about medieval life from many different sources. Thousands of medieval buildings still survive. These allow us to see the conditions people lived in. Excavations by archaeologists have uncovered details of ruined sites. Medieval art shows changing fashions in clothes and scenes of everyday life. However, the most important sources of information are documents and works of literature written by medieval writers. Most medieval documents and books are written in Latin. It was only in the later medieval period that it became common for people to write in their own national languages.

CHRONICLES

Chronicles are year-by-year records of events. Most chronicles were written by monks. An important example is the *Anglo-Saxon Chronicle*, which was written by English monks between about 890 and 1154.

LETTERS

Letters were the main way by which those people who could read and write kept in touch during the medieval period. Letters often reveal details of people's private lives that did not get recorded in chronicles. For instance, the letters of the Paston family, who were landowners in Norfolk, England, at the time of the Wars of the Roses (1455–1485), show the awful impact of the war on everyday life.

CHIVALRIC TALES

Stories about knights doing brave deeds to win the love of beautiful ladies were very popular. These stories are often set at the court of the legendary King Arthur, so they do not tell us much about how knights really behaved. What they do tell us is how people thought knights ought to behave.

For example, on October 27, 1465, Margaret Paston wrote the following to her husband, John:

Right worshipful husband,
I was at Hellesdon last Thursday and, in good faith, no one would believe the state of the place unless they saw it for themselves. [. . .] The Duke of Norfolk's men ransacked the church and took away all of the goods stored there, both those belonging to us and our tenants, [. . .] and they ransacked every man's house in the town four or five times. What they could not carry away they have destroyed in a most despicable way.

CHARTERS

Charters are official documents issued by the king to confirm legal rights, such as the right of a town to hold a market or a gift of land to a monastery. One of the most important examples is the Magna Carta ("Great Charter"). This was issued by England's King John in 1215 after the barons rebelled against his rule. In the charter King John agreed to respect the rights of his subjects and not act outside the law of the land.

POEMS

Poems were written about the lives of people in all ranks of medieval society, sometimes even about peasants. The stories in the *Canterbury Tales* by Geoffrey Chaucer (written about 1387) present an amusing picture of English society in the late medieval period. The characters in the tales include a knight, a miller, a cook, a lawyer, a housewife, a merchant, a doctor, and a sailor. They are all on a springtime pilgrimage to Canterbury and decide to tell stories—some funny, some serious—to pass the time.

THE DOMESDAY BOOK

The *Domesday Book*, a 1086 survey of land ownership in England, tells us a lot about medieval life. The survey was carried out by a team of bishops and barons. It records how many people lived in each village and how much land they owned.

MEDIEVAL EUROPE AT A GLANCE

TIMELINE

Around 476	Fall of the western Roman Empire.
793	Vikings from Norway and Denmark begin raids on England.
Around 800	Most of western Europe united under Charlemagne, king of the Franks.
886	The English king, Alfred the Great, defeats the Vikings.
962	The German king, Otto I, founds the Holy Roman Empire.
1066	The conquest of England by the Norman (French) king, William the Conqueror.
1215	England's King John signs the Magna Carta.
1314	The Scots defeat the English at Bannockburn.
1337	Beginning of the Hundred Years' War between England and France.
1346–51	The Black Death devastates Europe.
1429	Joan of Arc rallies French resistance against the English.
1453	The Hundred Years' War ends in defeat for England.
1485	The Tudors come to power in England.

RELIGION

Around 530	St. Benedict writes a rule for life in monasteries in England.
Around 1000	Pilgrimages become popular.
1054	Split in the Christian Church between the Roman Catholic and eastern Orthodox churches.
1095	Pope Urban II calls a crusade to recapture Jerusalem from the Muslim Turks.
1184	Pope Lucius III sets up the Holy Inquisition to prosecute heretics in Italy, Spain, and France.
1209	St. Francis of Assisi founds the friars in Italy.
1290	The Jews are expelled from England.

WORLD EVENTS

570–632	Life of Muhammad, founder of the Islamic religion.
634–702	Muslim Arabs conquer the Middle East and North Africa.
Around 1000	Viking Leif Eriksson becomes the first European to visit North America.
1099	Crusaders recapture Jerusalem from the Muslims.
1187	Muslim leader Saladin recaptures Jerusalem from the crusaders.
1206	Chinghis (Ghengis) Khan becomes ruler of the Mongols.
1271–1295	The Italian Marco Polo explores China.
1325	The Aztec Empire is founded in Mexico.
1453	Ottoman Turks conquer the Byzantine Empire.
1492	Italian explorer Christopher Columbus crosses the Atlantic.

FURTHER READING

BOOKS

Adams, Simon. *Kingfisher Knowledge: Castles and Forts*. Boston: Kingfisher, 2003.

Dawson, Ian. *Medicine in the Middle Ages*. New York: Enchanted Lion, 2005.

Gravett, Christopher. *Eyewitness Guide: Castle*. New York: Dorling Kindersley, 2004.

Macdonald, Fiona. *History in Art: The Middle Ages*. Chicago: Raintree, 2005.

WEBSITE

- www.bbc.co.uk/history/british/middle_ages/
  This website has many articles on different aspects of life in medieval times.

GLOSSARY

abbess head nun of a nunnery

abbot head monk of a monastery

apprentice young man who is being trained in a craft or trade

baptism ceremony in which a person is touched or covered with water to show that he or she has entered the Christian Church

bishop high-ranking priest who is in charge of all the churches and priests in a large area

catacomb underground burial place

chivalry code of conduct for knights

cog small, sturdy ship with a single mast and sail used for both trade and war

court (royal) place where a king's advisers and officials gather

crusade holy war fought in defense of the Christian religion

estate large area of landed property, usually in the countryside

fallow (of land) left uncultivated to allow it to regain its fertility

famine extreme lack of food for a very large number of people

feudalism system in which a knight serves a lord or king in return for protection or support

fief estate granted by a lord to a vassal (sworn dependant)

Holy Inquisition organization set up by the medieval church to investigate heresy (disagreeing with the teachings of the church)

Holy Land modern-day Israel and Palestine. The name comes from the land's connection with events in the Bible.

Holy Roman Empire medieval empire that was named after the ancient Roman Empire. The Holy Roman Empire included Germany, Italy, Switzerland, Austria, Belgium, the Netherlands, and parts of France and eastern Europe.

hulk large ship with a single mast used for both trade and war

humor one of four substances (blood, phlegm, choler, and melancholy) once believed to circulate in the body

journeyman trained workman who works for someone else and is often paid by the day

joust mock combat between two mounted knights

knight noble who fights in armor, on horseback. A trainee knight is known as a squire.

Lent period of 40 days before Easter

loaded dice type of dice used by cheats for gambling. One side of the die is loaded (made heavier than the others) so that certain numbers will come up more often when it is thrown.

manor village and its farmlands. A manor house is the home of the lord who owns the manor.

martyr someone who has suffered death for his or her beliefs

melee (in tournaments) mock combat between two groups of knights using blunted weapons

minstrel wandering musician

Normandy region in northern France

pilgrim someone who goes on a journey to a holy place as an act of religious devotion

pope leader of the Catholic Church

Renaissance period of European history beginning in the 1400s and lasting until the 1600s

secular not related to religion

ship's biscuit hard, bread-like substance that is made from baked barley and wheat

stylus pointed tool used for writing on wax tablets

tinker traveling metalworker who specializes in mending pots

tonsure haircut in which the top of the head is shaved, but the sides of the head are not shaved

vault arched roof or ceiling

wattle and daub small branches plastered with mud, used to fill in walls in timber-framed buildings

INDEX